Unitarian Universalism

Is a Really Long Name

WRITTEN BY JENNIFER DANT

ILLUSTRATED BY ANNE CARTER

Printed in the United States

Illustrations and text and cover design by Anne Carter

ISBN 1-55896-508-4
978-1-55896-508-9

Library of Congress Cataloging-in-Publication Data

Dant, Jennifer (Jennifer S.)
  Unitarian Universalism is a really long name / Jennifer Dant.
      p. cm.
    ISBN-13: 978-1-55896-508-9 (pbk. : alk. paper)
    ISBN-10: 1-55896-508-4 (pbk. : alk. paper)   1. Unitarianism—Juvenile
literature.   I. Title.

 BX9841.3.D36 2006
 289.1'32—dc22

 2006005562

5 4 3 2 1
09 08 07 06

The children's version of the Seven Principles on page 5 is by Carol Holst and the UU Church of the Verdugo Hills in California.

What's Inside

Welcome, friends! If you are reading this book, it means you want to learn more about Unitarian Universalism. Maybe your family goes to a Unitarian Universalist church and you have some questions. Maybe you have friends who are Unitarian Universalists and you are curious about their faith.

Either way, asking questions and looking for answers are important to Unitarian Universalists. We believe that no one is ever finished learning. Our faith keeps growing and changing like all living things. This is why we call our faith the **living tradition**. Let's go exploring and find some answers to your questions together!

Who are we?

Unitarian Universalism is a long name. Why? Because it combines the names of two different religions with roots that go back hundreds of years. **Unitarianism** and **Universalism** were both Protestant Christian faiths that had many beliefs in common. In 1961, they decided to join together to become one faith. Today **The Seven Principles** sum up Unitarian Universalist beliefs. What is the First Principle? (Hint: Look on page 5.)

Each person is important
Be kind in all you do
We're free to learn together
And search for what is true
All people need a voice
Build a fair and peaceful world
we care for Earth's lifeboat

All people are important, no matter what they look like or where they come from, if they're boys or girls, how much money they have, or what kinds of families they live in.

None of us is exactly alike, even when we live in the same family or go to the same school. Our differences make the world a better place.

It's not enough just to talk about what we think is right. We should work to make the world a better place. Everyone has the right to a safe and happy life. Unitarian Universalist children help people in lots of ways. They hold car washes, pizza parties, and bake sales to raise money to help people around the world. Older children help younger ones with their homework. Youth groups serve meals at homeless shelters. Children often lead the way in starting recycling programs in their own churches.

You don't have to be famous to do the right thing. You don't have to be powerful to make a difference.

What do we believe?

As we grow, we never stop learning about right and wrong. We learn about how to be the best people we can be. These ideas are part of what we call our **religious values.** Like children of all faiths, Unitarian Universalist children learn to practice their religious values at home, in church, and in their schools and neighborhoods.

Every religion has its own important teachers. Christians learn from the teachings of Jesus. Buddhists learn from the lessons of the Buddha. Unitarian Universalists learn from the wise teachers of many religions and from Unitarians and Universalists who came before us. We also learn from teachers today. New lessons and ideas are all around us. As we grow up and explore all of these, we find our own truths.

Sources of Our Faith

The sense of wonder we all share

What wise men and women have said and done

Lessons from all religions that help us
tell right from wrong

Jewish and Christian traditions that teach us
to love each other as God loves us

Science and reason

Religious teachings about caring for
the earth and celebrating nature

How do we worship?

Unitarian Universalists gather in **congregations** to share, to celebrate, to give thanks, and to work for a better world. In our churches, we hear words and music from many different religions. We also read the words of modern poets and writers. Most worship services have a time to light the chalice, a symbol of Unitarian Universalism. Our services usually have a time for quiet thoughts and for a prayer said out loud. This time begins and ends with music. Often we say a **covenant** together. A covenant is a promise we make to each other, like this:

> **We will be kind to each other and treat people fairly. We will respect and honor each other when we are gathered together and when we are apart.**

Who leads us?

Unitarian Universalist congregations make their own decisions and rules. The people in the congregation plan together and vote on important decisions. This is known as the **democratic process**. Most congregations have ministers. Choosing its **minister** is one very important decision a congregation makes. Ministers are people who help us live as Unitarian Universalists. They tell stories, sometimes called **sermons**, that show us what it means to be a good person and how religion can help us. Ministers help families when someone is sick or dying. They believe deeply that each person matters, and they remind us to believe that too. They help us understand that when we work together we can make a difference in the world. Ministers can help us talk about hard questions like, "How can I decide what is right and what is wrong?" What would you like to ask a minister?

Do we read the Bible?

Unitarian Universalists read the Bible and other holy books. A **holy book** is a set of writings about religious beliefs. For Jews, the holy book is the Torah. Some stories and lessons in the Torah are also part of the Christians' holy book, the Bible. For Muslims, the holy book is the Qu'ran. Some religions do not have holy books. They have sacred stories that tell about their beginnings, their beliefs, and their traditions. Unitarian Universalists also honor these sacred stories.

What is our religious symbol?

The **flaming chalice** is a symbol of Unitarian Universalism in the United States and Canada. Here's the story of how that happened. During World War II, many innocent people in Europe were put in prison. Even though they hadn't done anything wrong, they were punished for their religious or political beliefs. Members of the Unitarian Service Committee used the sign of the flaming chalice when they helped these people escape. Over time, the flaming chalice became a symbol of hope and healing and a way to remember that we all need to help one another. In many Unitarian Universalist congregations today, a flaming chalice is lit at the beginning of the worship. The flame reminds us of the spark inside all of us.

We recite a **Chalice Lighting**, like this one:

> **We light this chalice**
>
> **To celebrate Unitarian Universalism.**
>
> **This is the church of the open mind.**
>
> **This is the church of the helping hands.**
>
> **This is the church of the loving heart.**

Do we pray?

Many Unitarian Universalists pray. Some of us have favorite prayers we say aloud or in private. Prayer is a way to help us listen to our thoughts or to have a conversation with God. Prayer can be remembering what we are thankful for. Prayer can be naming things we are sorry for and promising to do better next time.

Praying regularly is one type of **spiritual practice**. A spiritual practice helps us feel the spirit of love and see what is mysterious and wonderful about the world around us. A daily spiritual practice helps us find a quiet place inside. Even things like listening to music, painting, and gardening can be part of a spiritual practice. Can you think of a spiritual practice you would like to do?

What is Sunday School?

We call our Sunday School **religious education**, or sometimes we say RE for short. It is one of the most fun and interesting parts of church. Our Sunday School teachers are special leaders who help us learn more about what it means to be religious people. Children get to ask questions and explore their own ideas about the world and about themselves. They learn about Unitarian Universalist history and other religions. They put on plays, talk about stories, and play games. They do projects that help others. Some activities are **intergenerational**, which means that people of all ages learn and work together. What would you like to do in Sunday School?

How do we celebrate?

When a baby is born, Unitarian Universalists honor the event with a **Dedication** or **Child Welcoming Ceremony**. Everyone in church welcomes the new baby and promises to help the child become part of the community. Children promise to be good friends to the new baby too. Many teenagers in our congregations go to **Coming of Age** classes to help them become grown-ups. At the end of the classes, the congregation honors these teens with a special ceremony. Congregations hold weddings and commitment ceremonies for couples who promise to love and care for each other and spend their lives together. When someone dies, the congregation holds a memorial service or funeral to remember and celebrate that person's life. These services and celebrations are **rites of passage** that help us share important changes in our lives.

27

Every Unitarian Universalist church is special in its own way. Some churches honor important dates in their own history. Others take a Sunday to honor animals or to celebrate their relationship with another church. In the spring, many congregations have a **Flower Communion**. Each person brings a flower to the front of the church, where they are gathered into a big bouquet to remind us that each of us is as different as each flower and together we create a wonderful community. Each person takes home a different flower than the one they brought as a reminder that the gifts of our church are always with us.

Unitarian Universalist congregations also celebrate holidays. Our congregations celebrate Christmas, which honors the birth of Jesus and reminds us that every birth is holy. Many also observe the Jewish holidays of Passover and Yom Kippur, and Pagan celebrations like Winter Solstice. What is your favorite holiday?

The living tradition of our Unitarian Universalist faith began a long time ago and keeps on growing today. Our faith helps us to remember how important each one of us is as we find our way in the world together. Being a Unitarian Universalist means believing that each of us is responsible for living a good life, respecting others, and caring for our world.

Thank you for letting us join you on your search for answers about Unitarian Universalism. Have a happy journey, and remember to keep asking questions!

FREDERICK WARNE
Penguin Young Readers Group
An Imprint of Penguin Random House LLC

First published in the United States of America in 2019 by Frederick Warne, an imprint of
Penguin Random House LLC, 345 Hudson Street, New York, New York 10014.

Manufactured in China

ISBN: 9780241355060

10 9 8 7 6 5 4 3 2 1

PETER RABBIT™

I LOVE YOU, MOMMY

the WORLD is BIG

and
I
am
SMALL,

But
YOU
LIFT
me **UP**

you're BY my SIDE,

To SHOW the WAY

and be MY GUIDE.

WHEN *I'm* FEELING

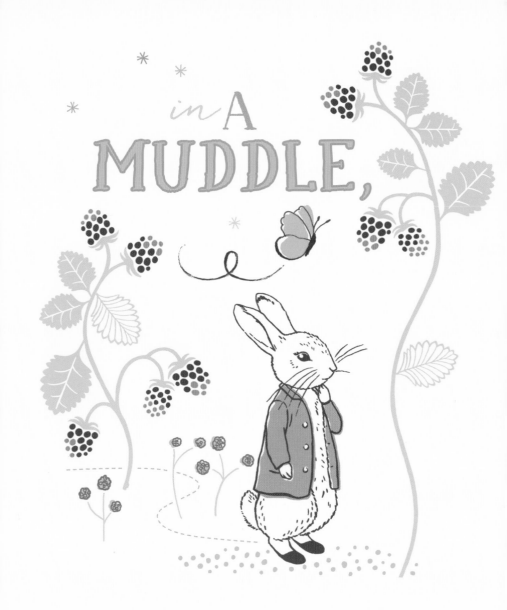

in A
MUDDLE,

Your
LOVING
arms

You
ALWAYS
KNOW

and
do KIND
THINGS

So as I
GROW

and
SPREAD my
WINGS,

what each DAY BRINGS.

like YOU DO,

and DEAR MOMMY, *I love*

you, too.